T0402821

THE NEW DEAL ERA

FOCUS
READERS.
NAVIGATOR

by E. A. Hale

WWW.FOCUSREADERS.COM

Focus Readers is distributed by North Star Editions:
sales@northstareditions.com | 888-417-0195

Produced for Focus Readers by Red Line Editorial.

Content Consultant: Katrina Phillips, PhD, Red Cliff Band of Lake Superior Ojibwe, Associate Professor of History, Macalester College

Photographs ©: W. J. Mead/National Archives, cover, 1; Library of Congress, 4–5; National Archives, 7, 12, 19; Nsf/Alamy, 9; Bettmann/Getty Images, 10–11; Robert Alexander/Archive Photos/Getty Images, 15; Lula Everidge's Family/Donna Vojvodich/USCG Historian's Office, 16–17; Red Line Editorial, 21; P274-1-2/Alaska State Library/Alaska Territorial Governors Photo Collection, 23; William J. Smith/AP Images, 24–25; Tami Heilemann/National Archives, 27; US Army/Department of Defense, 29

Library of Congress Cataloging-in-Publication Data
Library of Congress Cataloging-in-Publication Data is available on the Library of Congress website.

ISBN
979-8-88998-413-9 (hardcover)
979-8-88998-441-2 (paperback)
979-8-88998-493-1 (ebook pdf)
979-8-88998-469-6 (hosted ebook)

Printed in the United States of America
Mankato, MN
012025

ABOUT THE TERMINOLOGY

The terms **American Indians** and **Native Americans** are used interchangeably throughout this book. With more than 570 federally recognized tribes or nations in the United States, the usage will vary. Native nations and their people may use either term. The term **Indigenous peoples** describes groups of people who have lived in an area since prehistory. It may also be used as a shorter term to describe the federal designation **American Indians, Alaska Natives, and Native Hawaiians**.

ABOUT THE AUTHOR

E. A. Hale is a proud member of the Choctaw Nation of Oklahoma.

TABLE OF CONTENTS

CHAPTER 1

THE GREAT DEPRESSION

From the late 1700s through the early 1900s, US policies aimed to weaken Native nations. For example, some laws broke up tribal lands. Other laws required Native people to **assimilate**. Because of these laws, many tribes did not trust the US government. Yet, they found ways to protect their **sovereignty**.

Some Native nations pushed for change in Washington, DC, to protect their sovereignty.

The Great Depression began in 1929. During this time, banks failed. Economies struggled. Many people did not have money or jobs. This included Native people. Many of them tried to find jobs on **reservations**. But there were too few jobs. Families could not meet their basic needs.

In the 1930s, the US government started many new programs to deal with the Depression. This set of programs became known as the New Deal. One program was the Civilian Conservation Corps-Indian Division (CCC-ID). It created jobs on reservations. Tribes knew what was best for their own members.

The CCC-ID helped 85,000 Native Americans during the Great Depression. This rebuilt some trust with tribes.

They chose projects that would help their people. Some protected natural resources. Others cared for forests. Still more dug ditches for water flow.

Congress passed the Johnson-O'Malley Act in 1934. This act gave money to tribes. It funded schools with Indigenous students. It gave money to teach Native culture and buy school supplies. These funds helped students learn.

In 1935, Congress passed the Indian Arts and Crafts Act. This act protected Native artists. It said non-Native people could not copy Native arts and crafts.

REPORT ON BOARDING SCHOOLS

Many government-funded Indigenous **boarding schools** closed in the 1930s. A report shined a light on problems. The report showed cases of abuse and death. School staff harmed young children. The public learned of the suffering. So, Congress took away funds for these schools. Young Native children started going to public schools close to home. But some government-run boarding schools stayed open for older children.

The Indian Arts and Crafts Act supported Indigenous artists, such as Amanda Crowe. Crowe was a famous woodcarver of the Eastern Band of Cherokee.

They could not claim to be Indigenous. Only goods made by Native people could be sold as Indian-made. Native arts and crafts became worth more. Some artists created paintings. Others sold handmade goods, such as blankets or pottery. The act provided income to Native families.

CHAPTER 2

INDIAN REORGANIZATION ACT

Congress passed the Indian Reorganization Act (IRA) in 1934. This act fixed some laws that harmed tribes. It helped Native economies and preserved Native cultures. The IRA let tribes choose whether to accept the law or not. Many did, but others did not. Some did not like its policies. Some wanted more choices.

Some people called the Indian Reorganization Act the "Indian New Deal."

 The IRA provided new housing on some reservations to improve living conditions.

The IRA was meant to undo damage caused by the 1887 Dawes Act. The Dawes Act had broken up most reservation lands. Pieces of land were allotted, or assigned, to each tribal member. The Dawes Act forced Native people to give up **communal** ways of life.

The IRA aimed to protect Native lands. Earlier laws like the Dawes Act had caused tribal land to be sold, lost, or stolen. As a result, non-Native people now owned much of the land. The IRA let the US government buy back the land. It bought 2 million acres (810,000 ha) of what had been Native lands. The government returned those lands to Native nations. It also gave back other reservation lands it had taken.

The IRA tried to improve life on the reservations. It helped tribes create jobs for tribal members. The law protected cultural practices. It was now legal to hold ceremonies and dances.

In addition, the IRA funded loans to Native people. Native-owned businesses could borrow money. The loans helped the businesses grow. Then the business owners paid off their loans.

The IRA gave power to each Native nation. Each tribe could form its own

SOVEREIGN NATION CONSTITUTIONS

A Native nation's constitution may be similar to the US Constitution. But Native nation constitutions are different in key ways. For example, a Native nation may include religion in government business. Native nations use their constitutions to uphold their sovereignty. This sovereignty is older than the US Constitution.

Tribal members are citizens of the United States, a state, and a tribe. They have rights under all three.

government. The IRA also said tribes could create constitutions. These documents showed tribal sovereignty. But not all tribes wanted constitutions. The act said they could choose other ways to govern. In some cases, a group of elders chose how to run the tribe.

CHAPTER 3

WORLD WAR II

In December 1941, the United States entered World War II (1939–1945). Japan had just bombed Pearl Harbor in Hawaiʻi. The US military used the nearby island of Kahoʻolawe for target practice. Much of it was damaged. Although no one lived there, it was a sacred place to Native Hawaiians.

More than 44,000 Indigenous people signed up to serve in World War II. At home, 65,000 Native people helped the war effort.

Japan bombed Dutch Harbor in the Aleutian Islands in 1942. This was a US base in Alaska. Many Aleuts lived nearby. US soldiers made whole towns of Aleuts pack up and move. They forced nearly

HARRIET HOPE

Harriet Hope was five years old when Japan bombed her Alaskan island. Her family stuffed their clothes into suitcases and pillowcases. US soldiers took them to an internment camp. It was like a prison camp. They dealt with lice, measles, and the flu. They had to stay until after the war. In her 80s, Hope wanted the hard times to be remembered. She spoke about her experience. She said the Aleut people were patriotic. They gave up homes and lives for their country.

Many Aleut families left their homes by boat in 1942. Families were crammed into old buildings. There were no places to take baths. People hung blankets for walls.

900 Native people from their homes. The Aleuts were forced to live in places such as old mining camps. There was too little food. People did not have clean water. They did not have heat or electricity. Many people died from illness.

A large number of Indigenous people served in World War II. Of all ethnic groups, Native Americans were most likely to join as volunteers. Some of their training came from government-funded boarding schools. Being at an Indigenous boarding school was a lot like being in the military. The schools taught students how to fit in as soldiers. Students marched. They stayed in line. They followed strict rules. The US military valued their service in the war effort.

Native people helped from home, too. They built trucks, tanks, and aircraft. Hundreds of Indigenous women signed up. They wanted to serve the United States. They wanted to protect their communities. Some had attended boarding schools. Many Indigenous women moved to big cities to work. The jobs helped lift them from poverty.

BOMBING NATIVE LAND IN WORLD WAR II

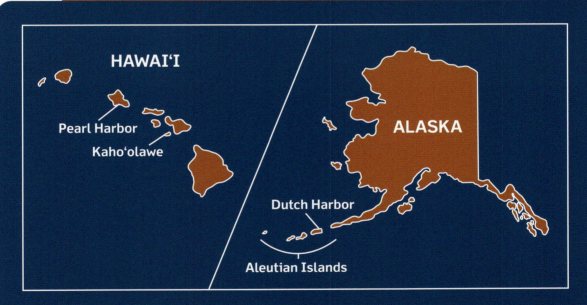

HAWAI'I

Pearl Harbor

Kaho'olawe

ALASKA

Dutch Harbor

Aleutian Islands

The US military bombed Kaho'olawe for target practice. Japan bombed Pearl Harbor and Dutch Harbor. Both harbors had US military bases.

ALBERTA SCHENCK

Many people know about Black Americans protesting **discrimination** in the 1950s and 1960s. But in 1944, Alberta Schenck, of Native and Irish descent, stood up to discrimination against Alaska Natives. The 15-year-old protested **segregation**. She went to the Dream Theater in Nome, Alaska. She sat in the "Whites Only" section. She was told to move to the Native section. She refused. The usher made her leave.

A day later, she went back to the theater. The theater wouldn't sell her a ticket. She got a friend to buy one for her. The ticket taker blocked her from entering. The two fought. The police came. Alberta went to jail. Her father paid the $15 fine.

Alberta sent a public letter to the newspaper. She wrote, "We are not able to go to a public

Alaska's Anti-Discrimination Act of 1945 was the United States' first anti-discrimination law.

theater and sit where we wish, but yet we pay the SAME price as anyone else, and our money is GLADLY received."[1]

Alberta's efforts helped lead to Alaska's Anti-Discrimination Act of 1945. This law gave all Alaskans equal rights to enjoyment of public places.

1. Alberta Schenck. "To Whom It May Concern." *The Nome Nugget*, 3 Mar. 1944.

CHAPTER 4

AFTER THE WAR

In 1946, Congress passed the Indian Claims Commission Act. This law helped Indigenous veterans returning from World War II. They had been of great service to the country. So, Congress helped them deal with land claims. The law gave them the right to sue the government. Lawyers helped the tribes with legal matters.

Leaders of several Ute tribes attend the signing of the Indian Claims Commission Act in 1946.

Tribes that won their cases received payments from the US government.

Despite these improvements, problems still existed. The 1950 census used the

NATIONAL CONGRESS OF AMERICAN INDIANS

Native people formed a new group in 1944. They called it the National Congress of American Indians (NCAI). Organizers wanted to build one strong voice for **Indian Country**. Native people from across the country attend its meetings. It has its own constitution. It protects tribal sovereignty and rights. It lends support to Native nations. The NCAI is the largest and oldest group that supports Native American and Alaska Native issues.

Members of the National Congress of American Indians attend a meeting in 2010.

P8 form to count Native people. This form asked more than the standard census form. It helped the government know if assimilation was working.

P8 forms could be used against tribes. The form asked for data on all people in each home. For example, what percent was their "Indian blood?" Did they speak or write English? Had they been part of any Native ceremonies?

In places where Native people were more involved in their culture, Congress believed there was a greater need for assimilation. Congress believed termination would help this process. Laws would end a tribe's right to self-govern. They would end tribal sovereignty. Native people would no longer be citizens of a tribal nation.

In 1950, the United States went to war again. More than 10,000 Indigenous Americans served in the Korean War (1950–1953). Many returning soldiers were proud to be veterans. They were

Mitchell Red Cloud Jr. of the Ho-Chunk Nation served in both World War II and the Korean War. In the Korean War, he sacrificed his life to save his troop.

also proud to be Native. Some wanted to take part in their Native customs when they returned. They pushed to bring back their tribes' cultures. Some nations held ceremonies and powwows. They celebrated the return of Native veterans.

FOCUS QUESTIONS

Write your answers on a separate piece of paper.

1. Write a few sentences explaining the purpose of the 1934 Indian Reorganization Act.

2. Do you think Native artists needed help from the Indian Arts and Crafts Act? Why or why not?

3. Where was the first US place bombed by Japan in World War II?

  A. Dutch Harbor
  B. Aleutian Islands
  C. Pearl Harbor

4. Why are Native nations also sovereign nations?

  A. They have the right to have their own governments.
  B. They are more powerful than the US government.
  C. Any US citizen may choose to join a Native nation.

Answer key on page 32.

GLOSSARY

assimilate
To shift to mainstream lifestyles and live like most other Americans.

boarding schools
Places where Indigenous students both lived and went to school, often far from their homes and families.

communal
Done together as a group, rather than as individuals.

discrimination
Unfair treatment of others based on who they are or how they look.

Indian Country
Native places and spaces in the United States, including reservations. It is home to hundreds of Native nations.

reservations
Land set aside by the US government for Native nations.

segregation
The separation of groups of people based on race or other factors.

sovereignty
The power to make rules and decisions without being controlled by another country.

TO LEARN MORE

BOOKS

Bruegl, Heather. *Boarding Schools*. Ann Arbor, MI: Cherry Lake Publishing, 2024.

Buckley, James, Jr. *Who Were the Navajo Code Talkers?* New York: Penguin Random House, 2021.

Rogers, Kim. *I Am Osage: How Clarence Tinker Became the First Native American Major General*. New York: HarperCollins Publishers, 2024.

NOTE TO EDUCATORS

Visit **www.focusreaders.com** to find lesson plans, activities, links, and other resources related to this title.

INDEX